IN THE FOOTSTEPS OF THE
BRONTËS

Mark Davis & Ann Dinsdale

AMBERLEY PUBLISHING

Dedicated to Emily

First published 2013

Amberley Publishing
The Hill, Stroud
Gloucestershire, GL5 4EP

www.amberley-books.com

Copyright © Mark Davis & Ann Dinsdale, 2013

The right of Mark Davis & Ann Dinsdale
to be identified as the Authors of this work
has been asserted in accordance with the
Copyrights, Designs and Patents Act 1988.

ISBN 978 1 4456 0779 5

British Library Cataloguing in Publication Data.
A catalogue record for this book is available from
the British Library.

Typeset in 9.5pt on 12pt Celeste.
Typesetting by Amberley Publishing.
Printed in the UK.

INTRODUCTION

It was established from early on that the houses and settings of all the Brontë novels had real-life counterparts. When Charlotte Brontë's *Jane Eyre* was published in 1847, it was described on the title page as 'an autobiography', and Mrs Gaskell's *The Life of Charlotte Brontë*, published ten years later, pointed the way. Gaskell's assertion that the Clergy Daughters' School at Cowan Bridge had provided the basis for the Lowood section of *Jane Eyre* brought her a threatened libel action. The first illustrated edition of the Brontës' novels, published by Smith, Elder & Co., appeared in 1872 and the commissioned artist, E. M. Wimperis, was supplied with a list of original locations provided by Charlotte's school friend, Ellen Nussey. It was announced in the advertisement for the new edition that the places described by the Brontës in their works of fiction were actual places. Even during Charlotte's lifetime, visitors had started arriving in Haworth 'on the wise errand of seeing the scenery described in Jane Eyre and Shirley'.

The Brontë Society was founded in 1893 and a strong topographical interest in the Brontë family's life and works is reflected in the papers and articles that made regular appearances in the society's journal. In 1902, the Brontë Society published Herbert Wroot's *Sources of Charlotte Brontë's Novels: Persons and Places*, and excursions to places with Brontë associations are still a regular feature of the society's activities.

The Brontë sisters did, of course, rely on their own experience and memories of places they had known in the writing of their novels. Charlotte's letters indicate that she would often take real people and places as a starting point for her fiction – to invest her work with what she called 'the germ of the real'. This is not to deny the Brontës their creativity, however, for Charlotte also insisted that 'we only suffer reality to suggest, never to dictate'.

The photographs selected here provide a fascinating visual record of places that are associated with the Brontës' lives and works. The inclusion of modern photographs alongside the old shows how in the intervening years some of these places have changed almost beyond recognition, while others no longer exist.

Ann Dinsdale
Haworth

St John's College, Cambridge

We begin our journey in 1802, when an ambitious young Irishman, Patrick Brunty, enrolled as an undergraduate at St John's College, Cambridge. Driven by ambition, he set about acquiring the education that would enable him to leave his humble origins far behind. This important new phase of Patrick's life was marked by a change of name, when he became Brontë instead of Brunty. It has been suggested that Patrick was emulating his hero, Nelson, who had recently become Duke of Bronte. St John's had funds available to assist poor men like Patrick to gain a university education, and his abilities attracted influential sponsors throughout his academic career, including William Wilberforce, the anti-slavery campaigner. It seems that Patrick had already decided on a career in the church, and St John's was renowned for its evangelical connections.

St Peter's Church, Glenfield

Following his graduation in 1806, Patrick was ordained and took up his first position as curate at Wethersfield in Essex. During his time at Wethersfield, Patrick fell in love with his landlady's niece, Mary Burder. When the courtship came to an abrupt end, Mr Brontë travelled to Glenfield, a small parish outside Leicester, where he had been offered a curacy. In the event, Patrick declined the curacy at Glenfield.

All Saint's Church, Wellington
All Saint's church at Wellington, Shropshire, was a modern building when Patrick Brontë took up his duties as curate there in 1809. The building has an elegant grey stone façade, with regular rows of large rectangular windows. During his time at Wellington, Mr Brontë met his lifelong friends William Morgan, his fellow curate at Wellington, and John Fennell, the master of the local day school.

Dewsbury Church

In December 1809, after almost a year at Wellington, Patrick Brontë headed north when he was appointed curate at Dewsbury church. John Buckworth, the vicar, was in poor health and the burden of the church offices was carried by Brontë. He was hard-working and ambitious, and came to win the respect of his parishioners.

St Peter's Church, Hartshead

In 1811, Patrick Brontë was appointed minister of the small Norman church of St Peter's at Hartshead, a post he held for four years. Mr Brontë's tales of Luddite violence in the area formed the backdrop to Charlotte's novel *Shirley*, and the evangelical Hammond Roberson, a former incumbent at Hartshead and friend of her father's, provided a model for Matthewson Helstone in the novel. The older image shows the building before extensive alterations were carried out in 1881.

Lousy Thorn Farm, Hartshead
There was no official parsonage at Hartshead, and for much of his time there Mr Brontë lodged at the rather bleak-looking Lousy Thorn Farm. The old farm, now known as Thornbush Farm, still survives but in a neglected condition.

Woodhouse Grove School

In 1812, a new school opened at Woodhouse Grove, Apperley Bridge, near Bradford. It was a Wesleyan academy for the sons of clergymen, and Patrick's friend from Wellington, John Fennell, was headmaster. Patrick Brontë was invited to examine the boys at Woodhouse Grove in the classics, and it was here that he met Fennell's niece, Maria Branwell. Following the deaths of her parents, Maria had left her home in Penzance, Cornwall, to assist her Aunt Jane in the school's domestic arrangements.

Kirkstall Abbey

It is believed that Patrick Brontë proposed marriage to Maria Branwell in the romantic ruins of Kirkstall Abbey, near Leeds. This medieval Cistercian abbey is set in beautiful parkland along the banks of the River Aire. In 1834, Charlotte Brontë made a pencil drawing of the abbey, probably copied from a print, which was exhibited in 1834 at the summer exhibition of the Royal Northern Society for the Encouragement of the Fine Arts, in Leeds.

St Oswald's Church, Guiseley

On 29 December 1812, following a whirlwind courtship, Patrick Brontë and Maria Branwell were married at St Oswald's church, Guiseley, near Leeds, in a joint ceremony with William Morgan and Maria's cousin Jane Fennell. Patrick and William acted as officiating clergyman for each other's marriages, while Maria and Jane were each other's bridesmaids.

Clough House, Hightown

Mr and Mrs Brontë probably lived in Patrick's lodgings at Lousy Thorn following their marriage. They eventually moved to Clough House at Hightown, nearly a mile away from Hartshead church, and it was here that their eldest daughter, Maria, was born in 1814, followed by Elizabeth in 1815. Externally, the three-storey house remains largely unchanged, although a plaque commemorating their occupation of the house has been set above the front door.

The Old Parsonage, Market Street, Thornton

In 1815, Mr Brontë was appointed perpetual curate at Thornton, near Bradford, and the Brontë family moved into the Parsonage on Market Street. It was here that the four famous Brontë children were born in quick succession: Charlotte (1816), Patrick Branwell (1817), Emily Jane (1818) and Anne (1820). In the early twentieth century, the frontage of the house was extended to incorporate a butcher's shop. After a chequered history, the building is currently for sale and its future uncertain.

The Old Bell Chapel, Thornton

The Brontë family lived at Thornton from 1815 to 1820, and during this time the seventeenth-century Bell Chapel was renovated and a cupola added. All the Brontë children, with the exception of Maria, were baptised here. In 1870, the church of St James was built across the road. The Old Bell Chapel was abandoned and now lies in picturesque ruins.

Kipping House, Thornton

The Brontës enjoyed a pleasant social life while at Thornton, centred on the wealthy Firth family at Kipping House and their wide circle of friends. Mr Firth and his daughter were godparents to Elizabeth Brontë, and Miss Firth was also godmother to Anne. Following the death of Mrs Brontë, Patrick proposed marriage to Elizabeth Firth and was rejected, causing a temporary rift in their friendship. Kipping House remains as a private residence, although it has been surrounded by modern housing. The older image shows Thornton in the early years of the twentieth century.

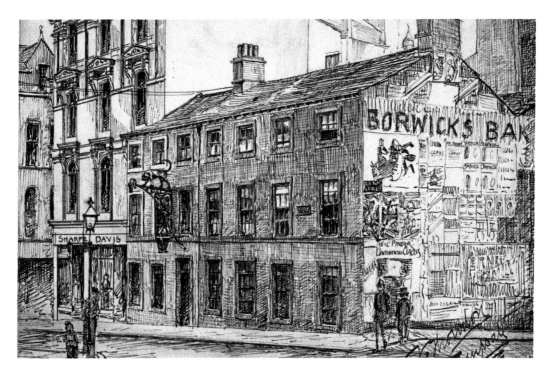

Talbot Hotel, Bradford

In March 1819, Mr Brontë escorted a large group of young people to be confirmed in the parish church at Bradford. The weather deteriorated and Mr Brontë arranged for the entire group to be served a hot meal at the Talbot Hotel, just off the top of Darley Street, before they set out on the 4-mile walk back to Thornton. In the late 1830s, when Branwell worked as a portrait painter, he lived at Fountain Street in Bradford (where he also had a studio) and would sometimes drink at the Talbot.

Haworth Old Church

The Brontës moved from Thornton to Haworth in 1820, when Patrick Brontë was appointed perpetual curate of the church of St Michael and All Angels. The exact date of the foundation of the church is not known, although it is often claimed to date from ancient times. The first reliable reference to a church at Haworth occurs in 1317, and it appears that a new church was built in 1488 and extended in 1600. In 1742, Haworth came under the ministry of William Grimshaw, a leading light in the Evangelical revival, and his preaching attracted such huge congregations that it became necessary to enlarge the church. The work was completed in 1755, and this is essentially the church the Brontës knew. With the exception of the tower, the church was demolished and rebuilt on the same site in the period 1879–81.

Old Pulpit, Haworth Church
The old church at Haworth possessed a high three-decker pulpit, which was used by both William Grimshaw and Patrick Brontë. The pulpit was removed when the old church was demolished, and for many years was left to languish in an old barn at the nearby village of Stanbury. The upper deck of the pulpit has been preserved and can be seen in St Gabriel's church at Stanbury.

Haworth Parsonage

Haworth Parsonage remained the Brontë family's home for the rest of their lives. Within a few years of their arrival, Mrs Brontë and her two eldest daughters, Maria and Elizabeth, had died. For the remaining children, their parsonage home and its Yorkshire moorland setting were a profound influence. It was where they grew up, where they began writing in childhood, where they wrote their great novels and poetry, and where they all, with the exception of Anne, died. After Patrick Brontë's death in 1861, the Parsonage served as home to four of his successors, during which time a large gabled wing was added to the house.

Haworth Main Street

Haworth mainly consists of the steep Main Street, a string of eighteenth- and early nineteenth-century stone cottages cut into the Pennine hillside. Main Street is cobbled with stone setts, which Elizabeth Gaskell tells us were intended 'to give a better hold to the horses' feet; and, even with this help, they seem in constant danger of slipping backwards'. The modern photograph was taken during Haworth's popular 1940s weekend.

Haworth Churchyard

The old photograph reproduced here is believed to date from 1860, when the Parsonage was still home to Patrick Brontë and his widowed son-in-law, Arthur Bell Nicholls. In a report published in 1850, the health inspector, Benjamin Babbage, condemned the Haworth practice of covering graves with flat stones, which prevented the access of air to the ground and the growth of plants that would assist decomposition. The trees we see in the churchyard today were planted in 1864 as a result of the report. Babbage estimated that over 41 per cent of the children in Haworth died before reaching the age of six.

Cowan Bridge

In 1824, a new school for the daughters of impoverished clergymen opened at Cowan Bridge, near Kirkby Lonsdale. For Mr Brontë, recently widowed and with six children to educate, the school must have seemed an ideal solution. In 1824, Maria and Elizabeth were dispatched to the school, followed shortly after by Charlotte and Emily. The school regime was harsh, and first Maria, then Elizabeth, was sent home in ill health. They died within a few weeks of each other aged just eleven and ten years respectively. Charlotte later immortalised Cowan Bridge as Lowood in *Jane Eyre*. Part of the school buildings forms a row of cottages, although the dormitory wing was destroyed by fire long ago.

St John's Church, Tunstall

Every Sunday, the pupils from the Clergy Daughters' School had to walk a distance of over 2 miles across fields to attend Tunstall church. It would have been a pleasant walk on a fine day, but in winter the girls would often arrive cold and wet and sit shivering through the service. An outbreak of 'low fever', a sort of typhus, took hold at the school and many of the pupils became ill.

St Peter's Church, Leck

The founder of the Clergy Daughters' School at Cowan Bridge was William Carus Wilson, who produced a number of publications that were in regular use at the school. One of these was *The Children's Friend*, which includes exemplary stories revealing a preoccupation with infant mortality, often accompanied by gruesome woodcut illustrations showing dead children and executions. The issue for December 1826 includes an account of the death of Sarah Bicker, who attended Cowan Bridge at the same time as the Brontës, and died there on 28 September 1826, aged eleven. Sarah died of an agonising inflammation of the bowels, and Carus Wilson's account concludes: 'I bless God that he has taken from us the child of whose salvation we have the best hope and may her death be the means of rousing many of her school-fellows to seek the Lord while he may be found.' Ill health was very much a feature of the school's early years, and at least seven pupils died there or were sent home to die. Sarah Bicker was buried in the churchyard of St Peter's at Leck. Also buried here are two other girls who died at the school: Mary Tate, who died of typhus fever on 14 August 1829, aged seventeen, and Emma Tinsley, who died of consumption on 6 June 1831, aged sixteen.

Cross-stone Church, Todmorden
After leaving Woodhouse Grove, John Fennell had worked in Bradford as curate, before being appointed to the parish of Cross-stone, high up in the Pennines between Hebden Bridge and Todmorden. Jane Morgan, Mrs Brontë's cousin, had died in 1827 and was buried in the churchyard at Cross-stone.

Cross-stone Parsonage, Todmorden
In September 1829, the four Brontë children, accompanied by Aunt Branwell, spent a few days at Cross-stone Parsonage with their uncle, John Fennell. Charlotte's earliest surviving letter was written to her father during the visit and describes how they spent their time 'very pleasantly, between reading, working and learning our lessons, which Uncle Fennell has been so kind as to teach us every day'.

Bradford

The Brontë family are very much associated with Haworth, but they also had numerous connections to the nearby city of Bradford. There is the well-known interlude when Branwell Brontë attempted to carve out a career for himself as a portrait painter there. As well as Mr Brontë's clerical connections, a surprisingly high number of the Brontës' friends and associates had links to the city.

Roe Head, Mirfield

In January 1831, Charlotte, aged fourteen, was sent as a pupil to Miss Wooler's school at Roe Head, Mirfield, where she met her lifelong friends Ellen Nussey and Mary Taylor. She spent eighteen months here, working hard and carrying away a silver medal for achievement. Charlotte returned as a teacher in 1835, taking first Emily, then Anne, as pupils. Roe Head has been extended since the Brontës' time and currently houses a special needs school, Holly Bank.

Brontë Waterfalls

The Brontë waterfall was a favourite haunt of the Brontës. In a letter written on 29 November 1854, Charlotte told Ellen Nussey of a walk she had taken over the moors with her husband, Arthur Bell Nicholls: 'Arthur suggested the idea of the waterfall – after the melted snow he said it would be fine. I had often wanted to see it in its winter power – so we walked on. It was fine indeed – a perfect torrent raving over the rocks white and bountiful.'

Red House, Gomersal

The Red House at Gomersal was the home of the Taylor family, woollen cloth merchants and manufacturers. Charlotte stayed here with her school friends, Mary and Martha Taylor, and the house served as Briarmains, home of the Yorke family, in her novel *Shirley*. The house is now a museum and the stained-glass windows, described in *Shirley*, are still to be seen in the dining room.

Rydings, Birstall

In September 1832, Charlotte visited Ellen Nussey for the first time at her family home, Rydings, at Birstall. Branwell, acting as her escort, was so impressed by the castellated house set among ancient trees that he told Charlotte he was leaving her in paradise. Ellen believed that Rydings had provided the inspiration for Thornfield in *Jane Eyre*. Although the house has been preserved externally, the internal features have been swept away and the building converted to a conference centre, owned by the paint company whose industrial units surround the house.

Bolton Abbey

The picturesque ruins of Bolton Abbey in North Yorkshire have attracted many artists. Charlotte Brontë visited the abbey, along with her family and Ellen Nussey, in 1833. The following year she made a pencil copy of Edward Finden's engraving of Bolton Abbey, which was exhibited in the summer exhibition of the Royal Northern Society for the Encouragement of the Fine Arts, held in Leeds in 1834.

Lodge Street, Haworth

In 1836, Branwell was initiated into the Masonic Lodge of the Three Graces. Throughout the period of Branwell's attendance, the Lodge meetings took place in this private house at Newell Hill, which has since become known as Lodge Street. Across the street from the Masonic building was the home of William Wood, the Haworth joiner. In his workshop on the second floor, Wood made several pieces of furniture for the Brontës, including their coffins. His aunt was Tabitha Aykroyd, the Brontës' servant, and in 1836 Wood and Tabitha jointly purchased three cottages in Lodge Street. It was here that Tabitha lived for a time with her sister Susannah Wood after she injured her leg in a fall.

Law Hill

In 1838, Law Hill at Southowram, near Halifax, was a girls' school run by Miss Patchett. Emily taught here for six months, and in a letter, Charlotte described her sister's duties as 'hard labour from six in the morning until near eleven at night, with only one half-hour of exercise between'. While at Law Hill, Emily is likely to have heard the story of its builder, Jack Sharp, a Heathcliff-like figure who attempted to usurp the property and fortunes of his adopted family – a story which may well have played a part in the creation of *Wuthering Heights*. Today, Law Hill and the old schoolroom, which stands opposite, survive as private houses.

High Sunderland Hall

High Sunderland Hall was a gaunt seventeenth-century mansion standing on an exposed hillside outside Halifax. Emily would have known the house from her time as a teacher at nearby Law Hill. One of the striking features of High Sunderland Hall was the carving that embellished the façade. Emily appears to have drawn on this architectural detail in creating Wuthering Heights. Mining in the area weakened the building's foundations, and although attempts were made to save the house, its ruinous state made demolition inevitable. All that survives of High Sunderland today is some of the decorative stonework, preserved at Shibden Hall Museum in Halifax.

Shibden Hall, Halifax.

Shibden Hall

Looking down the valley from High Sunderland is Shibden Hall, frequently claimed as the model for Thrushcross Grange, home of the Lintons in *Wuthering Heights*. Shibden Hall is a fifteenth-century timbered house that was inherited by Anne Lister in 1826. Emily's time at Law Hill coincided with extensive alterations taking place at Shibden, as Anne set about transforming the hall. Despite Lister's gentrification of Shibden, the hall remains a far more modest building than the Grange. Today Shibden Hall is a museum.

Top Withins

This ruined farmhouse, about 4 miles from Haworth Parsonage, has entered Brontë mythology as the inspiration for Wuthering Heights in Emily's novel. Throughout the nineteenth century the house was occupied by members of the Sunderland family, some of whom are buried in the churchyard at Haworth. Although it is possible that Emily had the moorland setting of Withins in mind when she wrote her novel, even when complete the house bore very little resemblance to her description of the Heights. Pictured is joint author Mark Davis.

Blake Hall, Mirfield

From April to December 1839, Anne worked as governess to the two eldest children of Joshua and Mary Ingham at Blake Hall, Mirfield. According to Charlotte, Anne found her charges to be 'desperate little dunces', and the obnoxious Bloomfields in her first novel, *Agnes Grey*, are said to be based on the Ingham family. Blake Hall was demolished in 1954, and the site is now occupied by the Blake Hall housing estate.

Stonegappe, Lothersdale

In May 1839, Charlotte went as governess to the Sidgwick family at Stonegappe, Lothersdale, near Skipton. Her time there was brief and unhappy, and in a letter written to Emily, Charlotte wrote: 'I have striven hard to be pleased with my new situation. The country, the house, and the grounds are, as I have said, divine. But, alack-a-day! There is such a thing as seeing all beautiful around you – pleasant woods, winding white paths, green lawns, and blue sunshiny sky – and not having a free moment or a free thought left to enjoy them in.' It is often claimed that Stonegappe served as the model for Gateshead, home of the Reed family, in Charlotte's *Jane Eyre*. The house remains a private residence.

Swarcliffe, Birstwith, Near Ripon

In June 1839, Charlotte accompanied the Sidgwick family on a visit to Swarcliffe House, the summer residence of Mrs Sigwick's father, John Greenwood. The house was pleasantly situated overlooking the pretty hamlet of Birstwith, but Charlotte was extremely unhappy with life working as a governess. The governess was a social incongruity; because she was middle class she could not be classified as a servant, and because she was poor and had to work for her living she could not easily be treated like a member of the family. A governess was often subjected to overwork and social humiliation for a very low salary.

Norton Conyers

During her time as governess to the Sidgwick family, Charlotte is likely to have visited Norton Conyers near Ripon, home of the Graham family, which was rented for a time by Mrs Sidgwick's brother Frederick Greenwood. Norton Conyers is one of several suggested originals for Thornfield Hall in *Jane Eyre*, for although there are no references to visiting the house in Charlotte's surviving correspondence, her friend Ellen Nussey remembered 'receiving from Charlotte Brontë a verbal description of the place and recalled the impression made on Charlotte by the story of the mad woman confined to the attic'.

William Weightman

William Weightman was curate of Haworth church from August 1839 until his death in September 1842. He became very popular with the Brontë family, and the sisters attended a lecture he gave on the classics at the Keighley Mechanics' Institute (*inset*). On learning that the Brontë sisters had never received a Valentine's card, he composed verses to each of them and then walked 10 miles to post the cards in order to escape detection. The sisters easily identified Weightman as the sender of the cards, and responded by sending him a Valentine's card in return. Tragically, Weightman died from cholera aged twenty-eight, and although his time in Haworth was brief, he made a lasting impression. The inhabitants of Haworth raised a subscription for a monument in his memory.

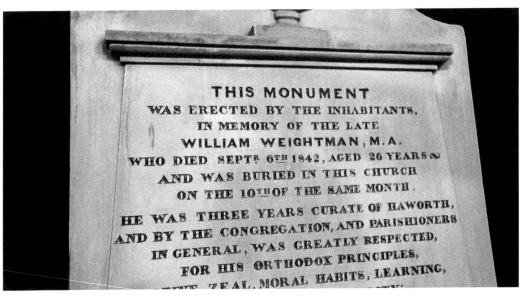

THIS MONUMENT
WAS ERECTED BY THE INHABITANTS,
IN MEMORY OF THE LATE
WILLIAM WEIGHTMAN, M.A.
WHO DIED SEPTR 6TH 1842, AGED 26 YEARS
AND WAS BURIED IN THIS CHURCH
ON THE 10TH OF THE SAME MONTH.
HE WAS THREE YEARS CURATE OF HAWORTH,
AND BY THE CONGREGATION, AND PARISHIONERS
IN GENERAL, WAS GREATLY RESPECTED,
FOR HIS ORTHODOX PRINCIPLES,
ZEAL, MORAL HABITS, LEARNING,

Easton House, Bridlington

In 1839, Charlotte and Ellen Nussey spent four happy weeks staying with Mr and Mrs Hudson at Easton House, near Bridlington (formerly Burlington). The Hudsons were acquaintances of Ellen's family, and during her stay Charlotte produced watercolour paintings depicting both her hostess and Easton House. She returned under less happy circumstances following the death of her sister Anne in 1849. Easton House was demolished in 1961 and East Field Farm now stands on the site.

Broughton Church

From January 1840, Branwell worked as tutor to the two sons of Mr Postlethwaite, at Broughton-in-Furness in the Lake District. Mr Postlethwaite, a landowner, lived at Broughton House in the centre of the town, and during his time there Branwell lodged at High Syke House. For a time, proximity to the Lake District and its associations with the Romantic poets inspired Branwell. On 2 March 1840, he completed a pencil sketch of the church at Broughton. The church itself has been greatly altered since Branwell's time, although Broughton itself remains much as it would have been in the nineteenth century.

Nab Cottage

During the time Branwell was employed as a tutor at Broughton-in-Furness, he managed to write in his spare time and sent samples of his work to Hartley Coleridge, son of Samuel Taylor Coleridge, who expressed admiration for his translations of Horace's *Odes* and invited him to Nab Cottage, his home at Rydal. Branwell was eventually dismissed from his post, allegedly for being 'the worse for drink'. Nowadays, Nab Cottage is run as a bed and breakfast business.

Lord Nelson
The Lord Nelson Inn at Luddenden was one of Branwell's haunts when working on the railway. In 1840, he spent six months working as clerk-in-charge at Sowerby Bridge, before being promoted further up the line at Luddenden Foot. A railway audit of the ledgers revealed a discrepancy in the accounts, and although Branwell was not suspected of theft, he was held responsible for negligence.

Thorp Green

In 1840, Anne Brontë went as governess to the Robinson family of Thorp Green Hall, near York. In 1843, it was arranged that Branwell would join her there as tutor to the Robinsons' only son, Edmund. Anne decided to leave Thorp Green and returned to Haworth in June 1845, followed shortly after by Branwell, once again dismissed in disgrace for 'proceedings bad beyond expression'. It is believed that he had embarked on an affair with Mrs Robinson, his employer's wife. Mrs Robinson was widowed shortly after, but when it became clear that she had no intention of marrying him, Branwell turned to alcohol to drown his sorrows. Thorp Green was destroyed by fire and the site is now occupied by Queen Ethelberga's College.

Little Ouseburn Church
Anne and Branwell attended Little Ouseburn church with the Robinsons. The church is situated close to Monk's House where Branwell lodged during his time at Thorp Green. Anne made a pencil sketch of the church in the early 1840s.

Monk's House, Thorp Green

During his time working as tutor to Edmund Robinson, Branwell lodged at Monk's House in the grounds of Thorp Green Hall. Branwell made a sketch, dated 25 August 1844, of the seventeenth-century building. The house still survives as a private residence. (*Above: Courtesy of The Brontë Society*)

Hathersage Church

In the summer of 1845, Charlotte and Ellen Nussey spent three weeks at Hathersage in the Derbyshire Peak District, where Ellen's brother Henry had been appointed curate. Hathersage is believed to be the original of Morton in Charlotte's novel *Jane Eyre*, and the church there contains several memorials to the Eyre family of North Lees Hall at Hathersage.

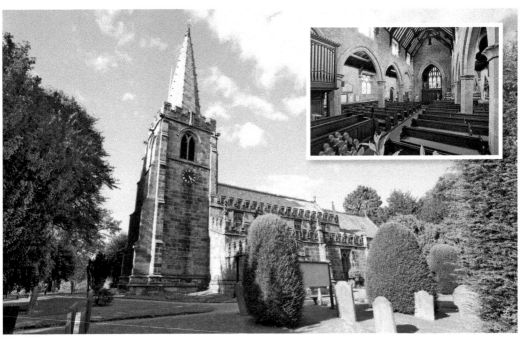

Hathersage Vicarage

During their visit to Hathersage, Charlotte and Ellen stayed at the vicarage, an eighteenth-century stone house that was being renovated in preparation for the return of Henry and his bride from their honeymoon. Henry had been casting around for a suitable wife for some years and had once proposed marriage to Charlotte. The extension built by Henry, which includes a bay-windowed sitting room and two bedrooms above, can be seen in these images.

North Lees Hall

During their stay at Hathersage, Charlotte and Ellen visited North Lees Hall, an Elizabethan manor house that was home to the Eyre family. North Lees is another contender for the original of Thornfield Hall in *Jane Eyre*, and it was here that Charlotte saw the Apostles' cupboard, described in chapter 20 of the novel. Nowadays, North Lees is divided into two holiday apartments owned by the Vivat Trust.

Moorseats

During their time at Hathersage, Charlotte and Ellen visited Moorseats, near Hathersage, which is believed to be the model for Moor House, home of the Rivers family in *Jane Eyre,* where Jane comes to rest following her flight from Thornfield. The house has been extended, and bay windows added, at some point after Charlotte's time.

Black Bull, Haworth
Elizabeth Gaskell claimed that Branwell Brontë's conversational skills earned him 'the undesirable distinction of having his company recommended by the landlord of the Black Bull to any chance traveller who might happen to feel solitary or dull over his liquor'. Despite the fact that alcoholism contributed to Branwell's death at the age of thirty-one, it was estimated that the consumption of beer and spirits in Haworth was well below average.

Branwell's Chair, Black Bull
The Black Bull stands close to the church at the summit of the Main Street and dates back to the eighteenth century. The unusual corner chair, which is reputed to be the one used by Branwell at the Black Bull, is now displayed at the Brontë Parsonage Museum, while a replica can be seen at the Black Bull.

John Brown's Grave, Haworth Churchyard

John Brown (1804–55) was the Haworth sexton and stonemason, and lived in the house adjoining the Sunday school. Brown was also Master of the Three Graces Masonic Lodge. According to Branwell's friend and biographer, Francis Leyland, it was 'no infrequent circumstance to see … Branwell listening to the coarse jokes of the sexton of Haworth – the noted John Brown – while that functionary was employed in digging the graves so often opened in the churchyard, under the shadow of the Parsonage'. Branwell painted a portrait of John Brown, which now hangs at the Brontë Parsonage Museum.

King's Arms, Haworth

The King's Arms at the corner of Church Street is one of Haworth's older inns. In the mid-eighteenth century, it served as the Manor Court. In 1841, the King's Arms was run by Enoch Thomas, whose brother William founded the firm of wine and spirit merchants close by. Enoch Thomas later became the landlord of the Black Bull, and he is said to have had his portrait painted by Branwell.

The Apothecary, Haworth

Opposite the church steps is the apothecary where Branwell Brontë is said to have purchased laudanum. In 1850, it was run by Robert Lambert who seems to have taken over the business from Joseph Hardaker, although it probably operated from less impressive premises lower down the Main Street at that time. Joseph Hardaker is one of Haworth's lesser-known literary figures, who published poetry in the 1820s and '30s.

Top of Main Street, Haworth

In 1850, there were seven public houses operating in Haworth, mostly within a stone's throw of the church. In the early image, the Cross Inn can be seen on the right while the Old White Lion faces down the street. Haworth has seen many attempts over the years to cash in on the Brontë name; the Brontë Café stood next door to the Cross Inn (not visible in the early image), and across the street a collection of Brontë relics were exhibited in the temperance tea rooms run by Francis and Robinson Brown, cousins of the Brontës' servant Martha Brown.

The Old Post Office, Haworth

The crowded summit of Main Street has changed very little since the mid-nineteenth century. In the Brontës' day, the building next to the church steps was an ironmonger's shop run by William Hartley, who also acted as village postmaster. In the 1860s, the post office moved next door for a time, into the building pictured here. It moved back again in the 1930s.

The Chapter Coffee House, London
Charlotte Brontë visited London on several occasions. Her first visit was made *en route* to Brussels in 1842, accompanied by her father and Emily. They stayed at the Chapter Coffee House in Paternoster Row. Mr Brontë had stayed here as a young man. The Brontë novels were published under the pseudonyms Currer, Ellis and Acton Bell. Charlotte returned here with Anne in 1848 on their visit to assure George Smith, Charlotte's publisher, that there was more than one Bell author. In later visits Charlotte stayed with the Smiths.

No. 59 Boundary Street West (Formerly No. 83 Mount Pleasant), Manchester
In August 1846, Charlotte accompanied her father to Manchester, where he was to undergo an operation for the removal of a cataract. They took lodgings in this house, and while her father convalesced in a darkened room, Charlotte began writing *Jane Eyre*. The site was badly damaged during the air raids that took place in December 1940, and the house had been levelled by 1945.

CHARLOTTE
BRONTË
(1816–1855)
In 1846 The Revd. Patrick Brontë came to Manchester for a cataract operation accompanied by his daughter Charlotte. They took lodgings at 59 Boundary Street West (formerly known as 83 Mount Pleasant). It was here that Charlotte began to write her first successful novel *Jane Eyre*.
2005

Brookroyd, Birstall

In 1836, following the death of Ellen's father, reduced circumstances had forced the Nussey family to leave Rydings and move into the less impressive Brookroyd. Charlotte visited Brookroyd many times and is believed to have corrected the proofs of *Jane Eyre* here on one occasion. Although hemmed in by a modern housing development, Brookroyd still remains as a private residence.

Wycoller Hall

Wycoller Hall, a sixteenth-century manor house near Colne, has become established in the popular imagination as Ferndean Manor, the house to which Rochester retreated after Thornfield was destroyed by fire in *Jane Eyre*. Although it seems likely, we do not know for certain that the Brontës ever visited Wycoller. In *The Life of Charlotte Brontë*, Mrs Gaskell recounts tales concerning the eccentric squire of Wycoller, which she may well have been told by Charlotte herself.

"Awaken o'er all my dear moorland
West wind in thy glory and pride." Emily J. Brontë.

THE ROAD TO WUTHERING HEIGHTS.

Haworth Moor

The moorland scenery around Haworth is particularly associated with Emily Brontë. Charlotte wrote: 'My sister Emily had a particular love for them, and there is not a knoll of heather, not a branch of fern, not a young bilberry leaf, not a fluttering lark or linnet, but reminds me of her.'

Ponden Hall, Stanbury

Ponden Hall lies in a valley about 2 miles from Haworth and is associated with Thrushcross Grange in Emily's *Wuthering Heights*. The seventeenth-century hall was home to generations of the Heaton family, traditional trustees of Haworth church and possessors of a fine library. The Brontës may have borrowed books from Ponden and would have been familiar with tales of past Heaton tragedies. Ponden Hall is a private house, carefully restored by its current owners.

Ponden Kirk

Penistone Crag, a rocky outcrop situated 1½ miles above Wuthering Heights in Emily's novel, was a childhood haunt of Catherine Earnshaw and Heathcliff. The Crag has been identified as Ponden Kirk, situated on the moors above Stanbury. A small cave-like passage, reminiscent of the Fairy Cave at Penistone Crag, runs through Ponden Kirk, and a local legend claims that anyone who passes through will be married within a year.

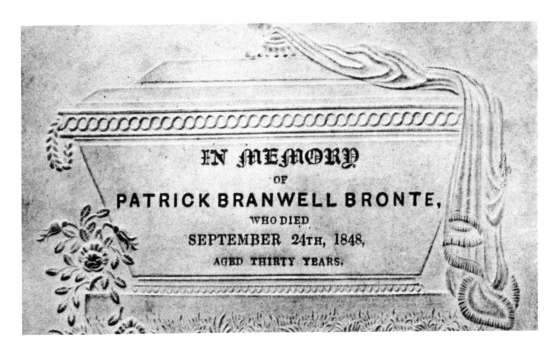

Branwell's Death

It is not known for certain if Branwell was aware of his sisters' success as authors. He died suddenly on 24 September 1848, aged thirty-one. Charlotte wrote: 'the removal of our only brother must necessarily be regarded by us rather in the light of a mercy than a chastisement. Branwell was his Father's and his Sisters' pride and hope in boyhood, but since Manhood, the case has been otherwise. It has been our lot to see him take a wrong bent; to hope, expect, wait his return to the right path: to know the sickness of hope deferred, the dismay of prayer baffled, to experience despair at last; and now to behold the sudden early obscure close of what might have been a noble career.' (*Above: Courtesy of The Brontë Society*)

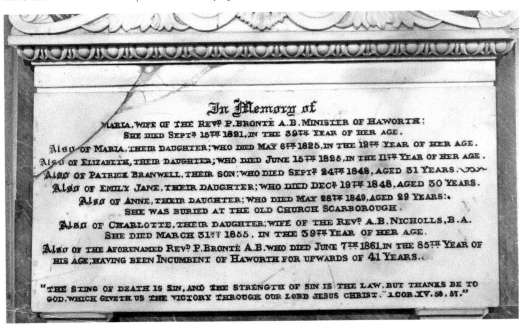

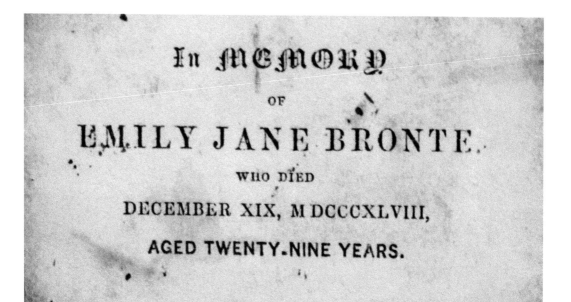

In **Memory**

OF

EMILY JANE BRONTE.

WHO DIED

DECEMBER XIX, MDCCCXLVIII,

AGED TWENTY-NINE YEARS.

Joseph Fox, Confectioner.

Emily's Death

Branwell's funeral is believed to have been the last time Emily left the Parsonage. She refused medical assistance and died from tuberculosis on 19 December 1848, at the age of thirty. In *The Life of Charlotte Brontë*, Elizabeth Gaskell described Emily's last day: 'I remember Miss Brontë's shiver at recalling the pang she felt when, after having searched in the little hollows and sheltered crevices of the moors for a lingering spray of heather ... to take in to Emily, she saw that the flower was not recognised by the dim and indifferent eyes.' Emily's dog keeper joined the mourners at her funeral and spent many nights howling at the door of Emily's empty bedroom. (*Above: Courtesy of The Brontë Society*)

Old Hall, Haworth

Haworth Old Hall was built in the late sixteenth or early seventeenth century and is one of the oldest buildings in Haworth. Situated just below the Main Street, it would have been a familiar sight to the Brontës. In 1920, the hall served as Wuthering Heights in the first film adaptation of Emily's novel, made by the Ideal Film Company and starring Milton Rosmer and Anne Trevor. Nowadays, the Old Hall is a public house and restaurant.

York Minster

Branwell and Emily had died within three months of each other in 1848, and it soon became clear that Anne was also ill. In an attempt to prolong her life, Anne travelled to Scarborough on the Yorkshire coast, accompanied by Charlotte and Ellen Nussey. Anne, Charlotte and Ellen broke their journey to Scarborough at York, and during their brief stay, Anne was keen to show Charlotte and Ellen the minster, which had made a lasting impression on her.

George Inn, York
During their brief stay in York, Anne and Charlotte purchased new bonnets and gloves. They dined and stayed overnight at the George Hotel, an old coaching inn in Coney Street. The inn has since been demolished and the site is now occupied by modern shops.

Scarborough, 1849

During her time as governess at Thorp Green, Anne would accompany the Robinson family on their annual holiday to Scarborough, a seaside resort patronised by the better-off northern families. There were many good hotels in the town, and the Robinsons stayed at the prestigious Wood's Lodgings.

Grand Hotel, Scarborough

During their visit to Scarborough in 1849, Anne, Charlotte and Ellen lodged at No. 2 The Cliff, where Anne had stayed on previous visits during her time as governess to the Robinson family, and where she died on 28 May 1849. The house was demolished to make way for the Grand Hotel.

Scarborough Castle

Scarborough Castle occupies a stunning location with panoramic views over the Yorkshire coastline. It began life as an Iron Age Fort, and would have been familiar to Anne from her visits to the town.

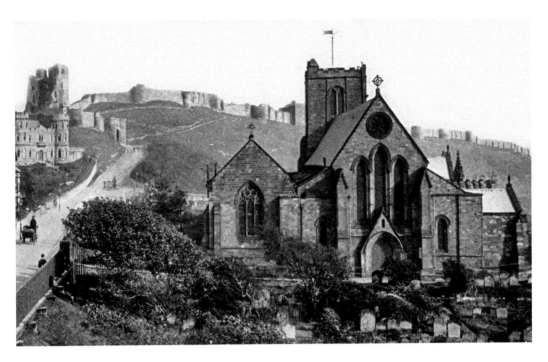

St Mary's Church, Scarborough

Anne had loved Scarborough, and Charlotte took the decision to bury her there, explaining:
'I have buried her here at Scarboro' to save papa the anguish of the return and a third family
funeral.' Anne was buried in St Mary's churchyard, high above the town. At the time of her death,
building work was going on at the church, so Anne's funeral service was held at Christ Church
on Vernon Road (since demolished).

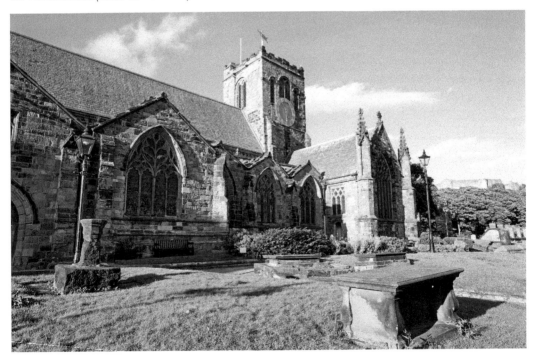

Anne Brontë's Grave, Scarborough.

Anne Brontë's Grave,
St Mary's Churchyard

Three years after Anne's death, Charlotte revisited her sister's grave at Scarborough. In a letter she wrote: 'On Friday I went to Scarboro', visited the church-yard and stone – it must be refaced and re-lettered – there are 5 errors.' One of the errors still remains, for Anne's age at death is given as twenty-eight instead of twenty-nine.

Cliff House, Filey

After Anne's death, Charlotte and Ellen found the crowds at Scarborough 'too gay' and moved to Filey, where they lodged at Cliff House. Cliff House is currently a combined café and shop, bearing a plaque to alert visitors to its Brontë connection.

Oakwell Hall, Birstall

Charlotte's progress on her second published novel, *Shirley*, had been dogged by ill health. Following Anne's death she immersed herself in her writing, an occupation that took her 'out of dark and desolate reality into an unreal and happier region'. Oakwell Hall, an Elizabethan manor house that Charlotte would have known from her visits to Birstall, featured as Fieldhead, home of the heroine in *Shirley*. The hall is open to the public and the interior was used as Wuthering Heights in the 2009 TV adaptation of the novel starring Tom Hardy and Charlotte Riley.

Gawthorpe Hall, Padiham

Gawthorpe Hall, the former home of Sir James and Lady Kay-Shuttleworth, lies just over the Lancashire border at Padiham near Burnley. Sir James was a medical doctor who had taken on the role of secretary to the Committee of the Council on Education. He had been forced to resign the secretaryship following a bout of ill health, brought on by overwork. The Kay-Shuttleworths were keen to make Charlotte's acquaintance, and she was eventually persuaded to visit them at Gawthorpe, which she described as 'grey, antique, castellated and stately'. The hall is now a museum.

Briery Close, Ambleside

In August 1850, Charlotte stayed at Briery Close near Windermere, the summer residence of Sir James and Lady Kay-Shuttleworth of Gawthorpe Hall at Padiham. It was here that Charlotte met the novelist Elizabeth Gaskell, then at the start of her career. It was a momentous meeting, resulting in a friendship that lasted for the remaining five years of Charlotte's life, and led to Mrs Gaskell producing one of the most popular biographies ever to be written, *The Life of Charlotte Brontë* (1857).

Fox How

Fox How had been built as a holiday home in the Lake District by Dr Arnold, the famous headmaster of Rugby, who died in 1842. Charlotte visited his widow and family there during her stay at Briery Close. Following Charlotte Brontë's death in 1855, Dr Arnold's son, the poet Matthew Arnold, wrote his elegy, 'Haworth Churchyard, April, 1855'. In the elegy he imaginatively places Charlotte's burial place 'In a churchyard high 'mid the moors', and was disappointed to learn that the Brontë family were buried inside Haworth church.

The Knoll, Ambleside

The Knoll, at Ambleside in the Lake District, was built in 1845 by the formidable social reformer and writer Harriet Martineau. Charlotte stayed here in December 1850 after having met Harriet in London the previous year. In 1853, Martineau's review of *Villette* hurt Charlotte deeply and caused her to break off the friendship. The Knoll has since been divided into two dwellings, although externally it remains unchanged.

The Old Sunday School, Haworth

The National Church Sunday School was built in 1832. The Brontës taught at the Sunday school, with Branwell being remembered among his young scholars chiefly for his short temper. It was here that Charlotte and Arthur Bell Nicholls entertained the scholars and Sunday school teachers to supper following their marriage in 1854. In all, 500 people attended and according to Charlotte, 'They seemed to enjoy it much...'

Grave of Tabitha Aykroyd, Haworth Churchyard

Tabitha Aykroyd came to work at the Parsonage in 1824 and, with only a few breaks, remained with the family for the rest of her long life. Tabby had been born in Haworth, and with a network of family in the area she had many tales to tell. On cold winter nights, the Brontë children would gather round the kitchen fire to listen to her stories of days gone by. Tabby died on 17 February 1855, aged eighty-four, and was buried close to the garden wall of the Parsonage. She was often referred to in the village as 'Tabby Brontë', and her gravestone records the fact that she was the faithful servant of the Brontë family for over thirty years.

DEATH OF "CURRER BELL."

In our *Supplement* of this day a brief reference is made to the death of this gifted authoress. The following just tribute to her genius and character we copy from the *Daily News* of yesterday :—

"Currer Bell" is dead! The early death [of the large family of whom she was the sole survivor, prepared all who knew the circumstances to expect the loss of this gifted creature at any time: but not the less deep will be the grief of society that her genius will yield us nothing more. We have three works from her which will hold their place in the literature of our century; and, but for her frail health, there might have been three times three; for she was under forty; and her genius was not of an exhaustible kind. If it had been exhaustible, it would have been exhausted some time since.

Currer Bell is Dead!
Immediately after Charlotte Brontë's death in 1855, at the age of thirty-eight, spurious obituary notices began to appear in the press. Acting on a suggestion made by Ellen Nussey, Mr Brontë wrote to Elizabeth Gaskell, requesting her to write an account of his daughter's life. Aware of the great public interest in Charlotte's life, he realised that inevitably someone would undertake a biography and it was his hope that an authorised account, written by his daughter's sympathetic friend, would put paid to some of the more speculative stories about the Brontës that were appearing in the press. *The Life of Charlotte Brontë* was published in two volumes in 1857, two years after Charlotte's death.

The Unitarian Chapel, Knutsford (Built 1688)
Described in "Ruth" by Mrs. Gaskell

Grave of Elizabeth Gaskell
Elizabeth Cleghorn Gaskell was the wife of William Gaskell, a Unitarian minister in Manchester. She had already published her first novel, *Mary Barton* (1848), when she met Charlotte Brontë. Following Charlotte's death, she published *The Life of Charlotte Brontë*. Elizabeth Gaskell died suddenly on 12 November 1865. She was buried in the chapelyard of the Brook Street chapel at Knutsford, Cheshire.

Mary Taylor's Grave, St Mary's Churchyard, Gomersal

Mary Taylor, Charlotte Brontë's friend from Roe Head days, led an adventurous life. In 1845, she emigrated to Wellington in New Zealand, setting up her own shop there. The business was very successful and she returned to England in 1859 with enough money to live independently. Mary also published articles on women's rights and a novel, *Miss Miles* (1890), before dying in 1893. Her younger sister, Martha, who had died at Brussels in 1842 while the Brontës were studying there, is also commemorated. Martha is believed to have died of cholera at the Chateau de Kockleberg, where she and Mary were studying. She was buried at Brussels.

Moor Lane House, Gomersal
Moor Lane House at Gomersal was Ellen Nussey's last home. Following the death of Charlotte Brontë, Ellen had remained in the Birstall area, where she was sought out by Brontë admirers, collectors and biographers, all eager to gain access to her memories of the Brontë family and her hoard of Charlotte's letters. Ellen died at Moor Lane House on 26 November 1897, aged eighty, and the sale of her effects was held at her former home. Since Ellen's time, the house has been greatly extended and now forms a small part of the Gomersal Park Hotel. (*Right: Courtesy of The Brontë Society*)

Ellen Nussey's Grave, St Peter's Churchyard

St Peter's church has been rebuilt since the days when Charlotte worshipped there with Ellen Nussey. With the exception of the tower, the present building dates from 1865 to 1870. St Peter's is said to have become Briarfield church in *Shirley*. Charlotte's friends Miss Wooler, the schoolmistress at Roe Head, and Ellen Nussey, were both buried in the churchyard.

DEATH OF THE REV. PATRICK BRONTE, OF HAWORTH.

THE last link connecting the Brontë family with the living has snapt asunder. The father of Currer, Acton, and Ellis Bell died at the Parsonage of Haworth, on Friday last, at the age of 83. He went down to the grave in the ripeness of years, and as the last of his race, his gifted children having all died before their father. Mrs. Gaskell, in her "Life of Charlotte Brontë," has given a sketch of the life of Mr. Brontë, from which, and other sources, we give a few particulars, reserving for another opportunity some interesting particulars respecting the Brontë family, kindly to be supplied by an intimate friend of the deceased.

Patrick Brontë's Obituary and the Brontë Vault
Patrick Brontë outlived his wife and all his children, dying at the Parsonage on 7 June 1861, at the age of eighty-four. He lived long enough to see Haworth become a destination for literary pilgrimage, and photographs of himself for sale on the Main Street. Mr Brontë's funeral was held on 12 June 1861 and was attended by hundreds of his parishioners. The burial service was read by the Vicar of Bradford, Revd Dr Burnett, and then Patrick Brontë was laid to rest in the family vault beneath the floor of Haworth church.

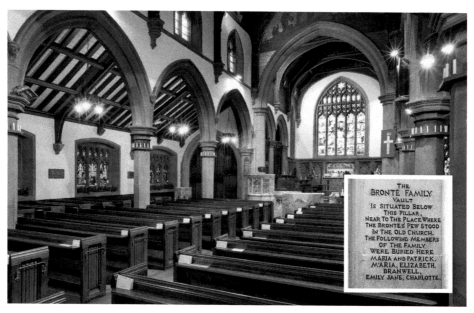

THE BRONTË MUSEUM, HAWORTH.

The Old Museum

The publication of Mrs Gaskell's *The Life of Charlotte Brontë* in 1857 generated a huge amount of interest in the lives of the Brontë family, and also created a demand for 'personal relics' of the famous authors. As those who had a sentimental attachment to these items passed away, a number of sales took place, and the collecting of 'Brontëana' began in earnest. There was a growing sense among Brontë enthusiasts of the need to preserve the surviving possessions of the Brontës before the opportunity was lost forever. The Brontë Society was formed in 1893 and opened its first museum two years later on the upper floor of the Yorkshire Penny Bank, now the Visitor Information Centre, at the top of Haworth's Main Street. The museum remained here for thirty-three years before the Society's acquisition of Haworth Parsonage. Today, visitors from all over the world beat a path to the Brontë Parsonage Museum.

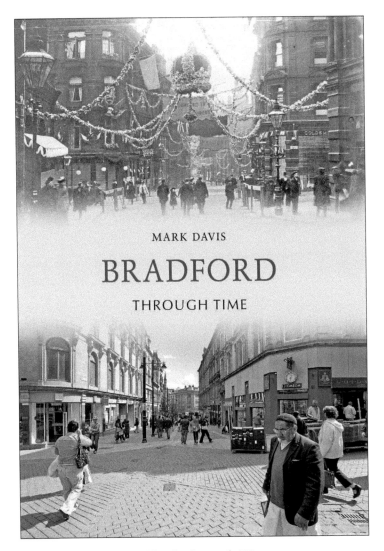

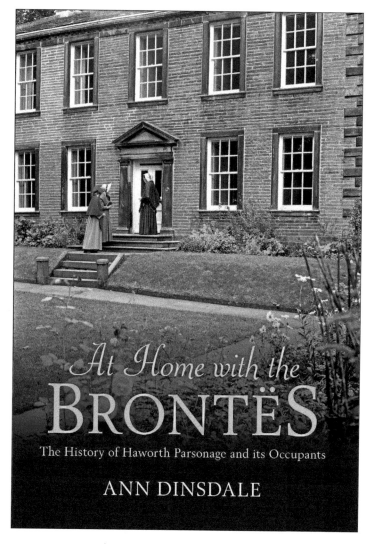

At Home with the Brontës
The History of Haworth Parsonage and its Occupants
Ann Dinsdale

The story of the world-famous home of
the Brontë sisters.

978 1 4456 0855 6
96 pages, full colour

Available from all good bookshops or order direct
from our website www.amberleybooks.com